THE SMOOTH YARROW

The Smooth Yarrow

SUSAN GLICKMAN

SIGNAL EDITIONS IS AN IMPRINT OF VÉHICULE PRESS

Published with the generous assistance of The Canada Council for the Arts
and the Book Publishing Industry Development Program of the
Department of Canadian Heritage.

SIGNAL EDITIONS EDITOR: CARMINE STARNINO

Cover design: David Drummond
Photo of author: Toan Klein
Set in Filosofia and Minion by Simon Garamond
Printed by Marquis Book Printing Inc.

LIBRARY AND ARCHIVES CANADA CATALOGUING IN PUBLICATION

Glickman, Susan, 1953-
The smooth yarrow / Susan Glickman.

Poems.
Includes index.
ISBN 978-1-55065-330-4

I. Title.

PS8563.L49S66 2012   C811'.54   C2012-901918-6

Published by Véhicule Press, Montréal, Québec, Canada
www.vehiculepress.com

Distribution in Canada by LitDistCo
www.litdistco.ca

Distributed in the U.S. by Independent Publishers Group
www.ipgbook.com

Printed in Canada on 100% post-consumer recycled paper.

For my mother, my brothers, and my sister

Contents

BREATH

IN THE GARDEN

"I will pick the smooth yarrow that my figure may be more elegant, that my lips may be warmer, that my voice may be more cheerful; may my voice be like a sunbeam, may my lips be like the juice of the strawberries. May I be an island in the sea, may I be a hill on the land, may I be a star when the moon wanes, may I be a staff to the weak one: I shall wound every man, no man shall wound me."

–From *A Celtic Miscellany: Translations from the Celtic Literatures* (1971) by Kenneth Hurstone Jackson

Homeopathic Principles

Witch's Tit

Not particularly cold, it blushes slightly, a tiny bud
in the shadow of my left breast. You'd think it a freckle
or a mole and not be as far wrong as those who
four hundred years ago
would have burned me alive at the sight of it
after, of course, a significant interval of gratuitous torture
involving spikes being driven into various parts of my
tender anatomy and ending not in confession
but in exhausted and probably unconscious silence.

But who convinced the witch-hunters that evil marks the flesh?
And who was *not* deformed back then by something or other—
the body a map of disease and malnutrition,
stinking, lice-ridden, with bleeding gums and falling hair,
eyes clouded by cataracts, lids drooping with palsy, limbs trembling with ague,
pocked with sores, tumours, abscesses and ulcers.
Yet they ignored clear evidence of our shared mortality
in their search for one singular blemish, an extra nipple
with which to suckle a satanic familiar.

You'd think that centuries of plot and counterplot would have revealed
that most successful villains are unremarkable, their bodies
as fallible as ours, their faces as plausible, their stories
as full of lamentation and excuse. That the hand of God
if it bothered to write to us at all would surely be less
inscrutable. But no.
The encryption of the universe continues beyond our comprehension
as we study the marginalia on each others' skin
blinkered and enraged, seeking somebody else, anybody else,
to blame.

Why the Wind Scares the Shit out of Me

because nature is meant to be background
to lie there submissively reflecting human endeavors
(a still lake under a red canoe, slight modulation of birdsong in the trees)
and not roar and argue and insist

because changes in barometric pressure give me migraines
because the smell of old cheese gives me migraines
because feeling guilty gives me migraines

because I keep my hair short, not having the vanity or steadfast
      concentration
required for good grooming and a truly feminine appearance
because the wind sounds angry, like the man who accosted me
at a poetry reading and snapped "why is your hair so short?"
and I've always run away as fast as I can
from anger

because no amount of abasement can appease irrationality
just as every ten metres below sea level adds another atmosphere
of hydrostatic pressure and the lower you go
the more intolerable the weight becomes

because it's taken me my whole life to learn this
because wearing a hat is a good strategy but yelling back
is even better

because I am as afraid of my own rage as of the wind
having no sense of entitlement, having spent my life being
equitable and sane, moderating the fury of others,
diving deeper and deeper despite the roaring in my ears

because I'm still holding my breath

On Finding a Copy of *Pigeon* in the Hospital Bookstore

for Karen Solie

I prowled the rows of the hospital bookstore with a fevered intensity;
"fevered" because it was a hospital, "intensity" because I was perplexed by
the mysteriously ruptured tendon in the middle finger of my right hand
in sympathy with which the whole hand had cramped
so that I could scarcely hold a pen or open a jar.
Even a five-month-old octopus in the Munich zoo can open a jar!

The octopus's name is Frieda, which reminded me
of D.H. Lawrence, and thinking of him
brought me to the hospital bookstore. It was minimally stocked
with anything resembling literature, offering those in pain,
afraid, or just dully waiting for test results
a choice of pink-jacketed chick-lit, cookbooks, investment guides
or glossy thrillers spilling blood
as red as that pooling down the hall in the O.R.,
as though emulating some homeopathic principle
of curing a disease by a parody of that which caused it.

And perched as eccentrically as the sparrow who sings from the rafters
at Loblaws, and looking just as lost,
was the only volume of poetry in the store.
Reading it I recognized at once what I disliked
about the bulky bestsellers nudging it from the shelf
like bullies in the halls of high school, their meaty faces
full of self-regard, their minds absent of thought.
I hate the omni-present present tense, that fake cinematic contrivance
meant to create a sense of "being in the moment" with the hero
as though life were a constant rush of adrenaline
with no possible mood but surprise.

Whereas poetry offers the results of its meditation
tentatively; it is not embarrassed to show that thinking
—some of it slow, arduous, confused—has taken place.
And then poetry doesn't rush ahead shouting, "Look at me! Look at me!"
Instead, it takes your hand, your poor mangled hand, like the good surgeon it i
and massages it joint by joint, feeling for the sore places.
And because it doesn't speak without reflection
you trust it, and let it cut you open.

Fracture

"What's broken can always be fixed; what's been fixed will
always be broken." –Jens Lekman

The frangibility of bone is a surprise even to those
who should know better. The mouth's startled "O"
is as apt for pain as song, all screams being soprano.
The body reverts to childhood in moments of fear.

"O" I said "O"
as my wrist split on the pavement, I felt the bones part
apologetically, they could not do otherwise,
being narrow branches not meant to bear the whole weight
of the toppled tree that was me.
And though the pain was far worse than expected
and something I prefer not to remember
the shame astounded me more.

That desires outpaces ability is an everyday disaster
but to be broken broadcasts failure to the world.
So that everyone who inquires, "How did you do it?"
has a momentary revelation of how tenuous health is
and blesses her own ordinary body
soldiering on through the daily maze
without falling.

"O" I say "O"
how astounding!

Down in the Mouth

"Every tooth in a man's head is more valuable than a diamond."
    –Miguel de Cervantes, *Don Quixote,* 1605.

Not bone but tooth enamel is the hardest substance in the human body:
hydroxyapatite, a crystalline calcium phosphate. It makes sense then
that my teeth are hard to please, demanding tribute of silver
and crowns of gold, distracting me with their incessant complaints.

I had my first dental misadventure at five, the same year
I learned to play the piano, its ivory grin full of song
a distraction from all bodily ills.
I remember hiding under the table and the dentist's arm
clawing at me, a mad instrument, his face incandescent with purpose.
His glee at the prospect of extracting an infected bicuspid
was more disturbing than the pain in my jaw
and easily trumped the allure of a bouquet of lollipops
blooming like tulips on his desk. (The dentists of my youth,
like pederasts, sought to quell suspicion with offers of candy
while doctors wreathed themselves in smoke to seem oracular.)

Since then braces and retainers, fillings and root-canals,
have ensured that my teeth are worth more than my collected works.
Had I been a shark instead of a poet I could have replaced my worn-out choppe
every two weeks; were I but a shark I would be rich!
Instead of consoling myself for a lost fortune by this nonchalant display
of the correct use of the subjunctive mood, my teeth—
or more properly their capital worth—
could have fed an indigent village, dug a well, sponsored an Olympic rower.

And what do they do, anyway?
Pulverize the occasional apple? Keep me from lisping?
The dragon's teeth sowed by Cadmus sprang into fully armed warriors
and helped him found Thebes and thereby western civilization.
My teeth just sit there and bitch.

Badinage

for Kim Maltman

Repartee is repair,
to wrap oneself in it a salve for the spirit
bruised by brutishness.

To wit: wit
is the whetstone of whatness;
whatever else it is
it is not naught.

A Conundrum

If someone tries to kill himself and fails and then tells you about it
is he really trying to tell you that you have failed him?
Can this be more about him trying to tell you that you have failed him
than it is about him trying to kill himself?
If someone tries to kill himself repeatedly and tells you about it repeatedly
have you failed him repeatedly or has he failed repeatedly
or has he succeeded in what he was trying to do all along
which was to make you think that you had failed him?
And anyhow, since he *didn't* succeed in killing himself,
have you, in fact, failed him? How? What could you have done
to keep him from not succeeding in killing himself except
helping him to succeed in killing himself?
Would this have been a success? For whom?
And what if he had really succeeded in killing himself—
how would you know that you had failed him
since he wouldn't be around
to tell you so?

Things From Which One Never Recovers

A 42-year-old eardrum burst in sympathy with an infant's infection
the arbitrariness of luck, both good and bad,
sunrise over a field of poppies south of Sparta
the boy in university who said *I'm sorry, but I only want to be lonely*
the girl on the high school basketball team who said
You have the biggest ass I've ever seen
the taste of cod-liver oil in a spoonful of molasses
administered by a schoolfriend's proper British mother
as a prophylactic against obsolete diseases
betrayal
giving birth
snorkeling for the first time in tropical waters—
how the fish part impassively to let one through
and carry on, oblivious to their own casual beauty
a contemptuous review that gets everything wrong in elegant language
like a sadist with impeccable manners
the entrenched injustice of the world that renders one's own problems
too trivial to mention
that there are different kinds of shoes for every sport
but only one pair of arthritic feet
Chopin's 24 *Preludes,* Opus 28
discovering the possibility of a really good wine
having a wild bird eat from your hand
being lied to by your child
seeing your child hurt and being unable to do anything about it
being hurt yourself and being unable to do anything about it

Homeopathic Remedies for Scar Tissue

The application of aloe vera to fresh wounds prevents the formation of permanent scars—at least on the surface. Nothing can be done about those formed long ago or buried deep inside.

Lemon juice will lighten blemishes of the skin. A few sips will also remind you how you got hurt in the first place, so you won't make the same mistake again.

Tie a handful of crushed mint leaves in a piece of muslin to extract their juice. Rub the cloth all over your scars. You may be wounded, but don't you smell fresh!

Mix sandalwood paste with rose water. Daub the paste on overnight and wash your face the next morning. (You should wash your face every morning, regardless; the fact that you are scarred for life doesn't exempt you from practicing good hygiene.)

If you don't have sandalwood paste—and who does?—any of the following are equally effective: olive oil, cucumber juice, green tea, or a solution of one tablespoon of sour cream, one tablespoon of yogurt, one tablespoon of oatmeal and a few drops of lemon juice. Best of all, once you have finished ministering to your pain you can eat the evidence.

Massage honey into the skin several times a day. An added benefit is that this practice attracts bees, who will teach you to dance in the sun and to fight back, even if it kills you.

Old Stories

Island

At bay:

where the world was while I
was thinking it, I being

adrift, then becalmed
castaway then
marooned

soft words for a hard place
that mind's island

rock amidst the eddies
with scarcely room for one—

or if so, a small one,
a girl and her book—

who now can find nowhere
to go that someone cannot
find her.

Rilke Doesn't Wear Sunscreen

but lolls in the hammock, his bare torso glistening
like that of a model in a Calvin Klein underwear ad.
He's waiting for an angel to appear, as one usually does at this time of day,
hovering over the monarda in the shape of a hummingbird
immaculate wings vibrating faster than the eye can see
sending out little pulses of chaos, fractals of indeterminacy.

Rilke clatters the ice cubes in his glass of Long Island Iced Tea
and rolls a blueberry along his tongue,
trying—not unsuccessfully—to extinguish his consciousness:
trying just to *be*. Everything is copacetic
until the angel buzzes in his ear, 60 beats per second, 3 grams of annoyance,
and forgetfully, he swats at it.

The garden grows dim with seraphic rage.
Rilke swings out of the hammock, faceplants in the mud,
pleads for forgiveness. Hailstones ravage the begonias;
crack the windshields of passing cars;
strip huge branches from the neighbour's trees;
pelt his sorry hide.

Sorry, he hides. But all-seeing, all knowing, as the Being is,
what's the point of that? So Rilke does the only thing he can,
given his abjection, his puny—but all-too-human—terror.
He hobbles over to the picnic table,
pushes aside the cheese-rinds and bread crusts,
a few grapes glistening with indolent wasps,
licks his dried-up pen to get the ink flowing
and writes a poem.

It just might be a good day, after all.

Shoes

They say that a pair of sneakers knotted together and slung across a telephone wire marks the spot where drug deals go down. You can see why that works: sneakers won't rot or melt or float away. They can't be painted over or scrubbed off like graffiti. But consider the first guy who threw them up there—did he trot off barefoot afterwards? Or had he, in his new druggy affluence, purchased expensive cross-trainers, the kind signed by celebrity athletes, and disdainfully pitched his worn-out ones away so that they got caught up there, *high*, a perfect visual pun?

No one has yet explained the litter of unmated footwear along city streets. Some specimens are sad as a new divorcée at a wedding but surprisingly few bear obvious signs of damage. The occasional perfect baby shoe is easy enough to understand: feet drum the stroller in a fit of rage or glee and goodbye, little bootie. But along the curb one spies a man's brown brogue in business-like condition, then a black rubber boot, shiny as licorice. What can motivate pedestrians to surrender one shoe and trudge on lopsided, grinding dirt into their socks?

Who knows? I have a laundry basket full of single socks. The streets are full of single shoes. The universe is a cabinet of mysteries we tiptoe by, wondering.

Hats

Hats just can't keep a straight face! They are the class clowns: the kids who get sent to the office for talking back and still get lead roles in the school play. Oh, they actually do their homework—in fact they never miss a trick—but you'd never know it, the way they slouch around looking idle, whispering nonsense in everyone's ears. This is why their sober and industrious brethren, the gloves, resent them. Even when there's a clear family resemblance, hats get all the attention.

But they need it. Being tethered to another's gaze keeps them from being blown away by every passing breeze: the slightest zephyr might do it. Because to hats, the world is indistinct as scenery glimpsed from a speeding train or remembered from some uncle's murky home movies. Because they want to be so much more than what they are. Because there has to be somewhere else bigger and better than here.

Putting on a hat, you wear your dreams on the outside, where other people can see them.

La Neige

pour Jacques Rancourt

C'est quoi ?
> Un tempête de plumes.

D'un oiseau ?
> D'un nuage sans littoral.

Plein de tonnerre ?
> Non, plein de silence.

Silence ?
> Comme une espèce de chanson.

Pour une voix, ou plusieurs ?
> Plusieurs. C'est une danse des êtres éphémères

Mais vous avez dit que c'était une chanson.
> Je voulais dire une danse. Le silence lui-même, en marche.

Où ?
> À la frontière.

La frontière de quoi ?
> Là où la terre et le ciel se rencontrent.

L'horizon ?
> L'horizon.

Ce n'est peut-être rien que du sable.
> Ça peut n'être rien, mais ce n'est pas du sable.

Qu'est ce que ça veut dire, *rien* ?
> Ses paysages sont illusoires.

Est-ce que vous pouvez y construire ?
> Quand c'est assez mouillé.

Et quand ce n'est pas mouillé, qu'est-ce qui se passe ?
> Ça se fracasse sous pied, ou ça se durcit dans une dangereuse
transparence.

Comme du verre ?

Mais sans reflet.
En mouvement, comme une rivière ?
Sans mouvement. Comme un lac.
De l'eau alors ?
Alors de l'eau.

Snow

for Helen Dunmore

What is it?
  A storm of feathers
From a bird?
  From a landlocked cloud.
Full of thunder?
  No, full of silence.
Silence?
  As a kind of a song.
For one voice or many?
  Many. It is a dance of transient beings.
But you said it was a song.
  I meant a dance. Silence itself, moving.
Where?
  To the edge.
The edge of what?
  Where earth and sky meet.
The horizon?
  The horizon.
Perhaps it is nothing but sand.
  It may be nothing, but it is not sand.
What do you mean, *nothing*?
  Its landscapes are illusory.
Can you build with it?
  When it is wet enough.
And when it is not wet, what then?
  It cracks underfoot, or hardens into dangerous transparency.
Like glass?
  But without reflection.
Moving like a river?
  Unmoving. Like a lake.
Water then.
  Then water.

Average Life

for Sheldon Zitner

In the OED
it comes between *hearse* and *hearth*.
Cognates include *heart-ache, heart-break, heart-burn,*
heartless, heart's ease, heart-rending,
heart-whole and *heart-wise*.

In the embryo, it maps the species' evolution:
a tube at first, fit for a fish,
then two-chambered and frog-like,
then a turtle's unshelled three.

310 grams, no bigger than a fist,
it pumps 4,300 gallons a day,
beats 2½ billion times
in an average life.

Eventually it may be replaced by a battery.
Barney Clark survived 112 days
on forced air and polyester; a baboon's heart
massaged Baby Fae
for three brief weeks.

Four red rooms
plush, and full of music
hiding in the chest's thicket.

Tap and listen:
is anyone home?

Stray

This All Hallow's cat, fiery orange and black,
her back a starved landscape, fur alive with fleas,
pleases me. We stare candidly into each other's eyes,
green into greener, making contented noises in our bellies.

Hers prefers tuna, disdaining dog-kibble
and also the dog, who resents her presence on our porch
and in my attention. *One pet is enough for any family!*
he growls and my husband, sadly, agrees.

So the stray waits, between saucers of milk and midnight saunters,
for her real people to find her. But they don't. They don't post ads
or answer mine and finally it's just too cold for anyone's comfort.
A house-cat after all, she wants in—

rubs expectantly against my legs each time the door opens
and shuts again, leaving her outside.
I can't leave her outside anymore; wrap her narrow body
purring, purring, in a blanket in my arms
then in a box in the car

and drop her at the shelter;
another betrayal.

Jam

My father fished, my mother made jam.
The primal order of things, those Augusts in the country.

Along the dirt road to the fishing camp
our fingers bleeding with juice
we kids picked raspberries, useful for once;
for once understanding why we were here.

Crickets singing in the grass,
quick snakes in the underbrush—
forgotten things, remembered again.

The jam simmered.
It simmered on the wood stove for hours, thickening.
Spilled sugar crackled underfoot
and the cabin got hotter and hotter.

My mother's black hair stuck to her forehead as she stirred the pot;
she heaved it up and ladled the sweetness into jars
sealed them with paraffin wax the way our faces in photographs
have sealed those summers:

nothing but sugar preserved, no memory
of the boiling.

The Dog at the End of the Bed

That we are our bodies frees us
and makes us strange. Strangers
who moments ago were bored, terribly bored,
discussing taxes, teachers, where to buy electronics—
bored with life and each other and now again
it's new.

Or almost new.
I know what you like best, and when,
as you do for me
and you do for me
what no one else has, my dear.

So we are memory & flesh—
memory and flesh and distance

for even here, now,
the singularity remains. Relentless,
amused and ageless, lonely,
waiting for the fuss to be over, the untangling
of arms and legs and breasts etcetera

waiting and watching
like a dog at the end of the bed.

Kiss

The baby, insatiable, eats you,
your cheek round as a breast
and almost as soft.

He pats it as a baker pats dough—
part scientist, part lover.

The dog licks his ass
and then your face;

nature's egalitarian,
he means it kindly.

Mouth to mouth
we find each others' softest places
and breathe.

Old Stories

The Lion pursues the Virgin, her white dress
a transparent veil
flickering before the red cave of his jaws.
Scorpion's sting grazes the Archer's fugitive heels
while the Fish scull languorously
into unfathomable space.

Just connect the dots and you'll find them
there and *there,* waiting
with a remorseless patience
for us to look up
past flickering city lights and out of
our element,

slack-jawed yokels, pointing
at those few stars that shoot, or fall
—which, we'll never know—
and thus escape even
the oldest narratives.

Yarrow

Faded, bent, and obdurate
its yellowing lace deceptive
the delicacy of old ladies who survive their mates

to work on in the garden
season after season
with arthritic fingers

who know the names of all winged visitors
and can recognize their songs across the twilight
as the nicotiana releases its scent

who plant verbena, penstemon, lobelia and monarda
for the butterflies and birds
and David Austin roses for themselves

who do not deadhead the sunflowers
so the creatures will have something to eat
who keep cats, but never set mousetraps

who use their best china every day
and jump the queue at the grocery store
because they have so little in their baskets
and no more time to waste

Untitled

Prayer has never been my way
so when the brain stalls in these sad latitudes
when nothing comes of nothing but more grief
I'm stuck.

No one to ask for help.
No one to blame.

The busy world churns on without a backward glance
not that everyone else is rapt in praise
of the quotidian, or deeply happy just to be here, but they
keep right on going, leaving the fallen where they fall.

And I am knackered; can't jolly myself into admiration
for the spendthrift gold of October's trees
or the whatnots of whatever;
frankly, I no longer care

skewered on the truth these lidless eyes cannot shut out:
my time's too short, my work too slight
to matter.

Jacob's Ladder

On the narrow staircase carved into rock at Ein Avdat
tourists pass each other like the angels
on Jacob's ladder; some climbing up, some down.
There's rarely a level path in this land
but if you watch your feet you are as likely to tumble
as if you don't, so just keep going and
someone might take your hand.

The ibex observe us curiously,
their four legs steadier than our two,
and above them the layered cliffs are scarred
with caves emptied of human presence
and bones gnawed by jackals.
The cliffs build towards a sky
that's seen it all before, and will again, and doesn't care.

A few thorny trees bear aromatic fruit: the balm mentioned in the Torah.
Everything here is mentioned in the Torah so that
what once seemed merely myth becomes embodied
folding now into then
and us into them, the ancestors,
who loom higher than the cliffs, their shadows
the shadows of clouds, their memory
the memory of clouds

passing and repassing in the high desert skies
letting fall a rare and welcome rain;
filling the wadis with green.
My heart is full.
My legs tremble with fatigue, but I have
the smell of the Dead Sea in my hair
and a stone for my father's grave
in my pocket.

Breath

Breath

Walking the dog in Cedarvale Ravine on a grey October morning
it is precisely the lack of sunlight that suffuses the air with something
indefinable; that whets the gold of each leaf,
brightens the blue chicory starring the overgrown grass
and makes old hounds frolic like pups—

the same gathering radiance that flares before thunder
except that here
is only a small rain, aromatic as cider,
a kind of vertical mist, making the half-full glass of autumn brim over

with glory. Not an upper case, grandiose kind of Glory
but a halo tossed like a Frisbee, accidental and luminescent,
so that the dog runs mad ellipses in a delirium of pleasure
then lifts his leg to mark it as his own
and I just stand for one tranced moment
breathing the trees that breathe us

until time reels back through itself
like a dog chasing his tail
and the moment evaporates
and we are only in the park, walking,
a middle-aged lady and her wet and dirty dog
to all outward appearances unchanged by

whatever just happened
but never unchanged, although
our allowance of grace is paid in
such small increments.

~

Such mysteries are daily as breath
or bread, but their meaning
remains intractable:

the maple tree's self-immolation,
a white butterfly hatching
before the snow has fully melted

~

First memory: my father inconsolable
at his mother's funeral.
Or no, that could not have been the first
because I do remember her smell
of lavender, that capacious lap.
She read me a book about a duck

then left without saying goodbye
and after her, a parade of others, mostly old
but not always; never old enough.
So many sleepless nights
I've counted lovers, sleepless nights
I've counted houses, sleepless
nights I've counted deaths

fingers rippling to keep track
as though accompanying a silent movie
with silent music.

~

I watched my father die
though I did not get to hold him
as I have held too many pets
in their last moments.
Their lives were so much shorter than his;
their dying proportionately longer.
Does that mean they suffered more?

Limbs stiffened, shaken by spasms.
Warm fur cooled in my ineffectual hands.
I kissed them as though it mattered,
abashed at the extreme inwardness
such small bodies could attain——

the same privacy that gripped my father
in a room full of sobbing relatives,
a room I hated being dragged to, which felt obscene to me
despite my people's belief that it wasn't voyeurism
but generosity to crowd around his bed
because no one should have to die alone.

~

Once there was a dead cat in my neighbour's yard.
For days its stench had soiled the air, untraceable.
Only as it started to lessen, becoming
not a noxious cloud but a trail my nose could follow,
did I locate the spruce tree it had crawled under
craving solitude at the end.

The second time I smelled that smell
it came from a decomposing drunk
who'd found shelter in an abandoned car
and died there one bitter winter night.

I would be the same, I think.
I think my father was too.
I think the mourners' melodrama distracted him
from the business at hand.
I think he needed us to go away, but we wouldn't,
so he had to leave first.

~

When my father was dying we studied his breath:
it came rapidly and laboured and then
not at all.

We were stunned by his silence.
We started to gather our goodbyes into it;
keeping vigil there we began to relent and let him go.
We finally exhaled, we began to weep,

but then the breath surged in his throat
and came rattling out again.
It reached out to us but we did not reach back.

We hesitated, no longer sure what to pray for.

In the Garden

In the Garden

~

Little green caterpillars were eating my rosebuds.
I asked the horticulturist what they were called and she said
"I just call them little green caterpillars."

Furious, the goldfinch
scolds from the cedar. We top up the feeder with seed
and keep out of his way.

His cosmology must teem with obedient demons
lurking, clumsy and pathetic,
in his peripheral vision.

I squished the caterpillars by hand.
To them, I am a vengeful god.

~

In their larval stage butterflies
are destructive,
all sinuous appetite on invisible legs,
but full-fledged they sip nectar daintily,
fanning wings finer than the
almost-transparent blossoms
of blue campanula
pooled at their feet.

So I bargain with them
as one does with all fierce creatures:
Don't kill my babies and
I won't kill yours.

~

This winter's losses:
one moonbeam coreopsis, two astilbe, a Japanese fern
and a shade-loving yew that should have done better.
The ledger balanced by self-seeding mysotis, mallow and dill;
sunny euphorbia and purple vetch.

On balance, a balance
I can live with. The losses were costlier than the gains
but isn't that always the way? Meanwhile the garden
goes on endlessly improvising;
climbing roses that never bloomed before a white cataract
over the fence and the unfailing rudebekia
failing.

~

To lure the ruby-throated hummingbird
I planted monarda. It didn't take
but the bird still visits from time to time,
a transient vision.

To drive the black cat from the bushes
I sprayed him with the hose.
Hissing defiance,
he continues to stalk the feeder.

Like poets, gardeners
never concede failure.
If something doesn't thrive
they promptly transplant it

and obsessed with pruning
they rise at dawn
while honest folk still sleep
to savage what they've made.

~

(found poem about certain potentially dangerous plants in my garden)

Horses have been poisoned in Japan
by ingesting the leaves of chive
in early spring.

In the Netherlands during the Second World War
starving cattle were fed daffodil bulbs
and fatally poisoned.

Though livestock in Nova Scotia seem unaffected
by grazing lupines
their milk becomes poisonous.

Ingesting large quantities of lily-of-the-valley
can cause problems to family pets
such as cats and dogs.

Scilla is not a good plant
to have around children or pets
which have a habit of chewing leaves.

Poppy seeds are harmless and edible
but all other parts of the poppy
contain toxins.

Bleeding heart may be a threat
if children are tempted to eat the showy, white or pink
heart-shaped blossoms.

~

The showy, white or pink
heart-shaped blossoms
for all their delicacy
withstand the windiest weather

but the upright spears of delphinium
are defeated
by a single night
of summer rain

The flowers I love best
—peonies, irises, poppies—
are transient as twilight
but the garden gathers them up in huge
ebullient armfuls
like a father lofting his child.

Some say the garden is all about survival,
survival and sacrifice
(dogwood dipping silver blades
in the blood of the Japanese maple,
armature of honeysuckle buttressing
a sickly clematis),

but that's not why I love it. I love it
because it is unpredictable
because it takes my tentative little efforts
and riffs them into a fat sassy jazz
I didn't know I had in me.
Because it doesn't hold back.
Because it says *Fuck you* to decorum and
Fuck me

to all the butterflies.

~

Like the bumble bee
I am partial to blue flowers.
In my garden, chinodoxia
politely clears the snow for scilla;
scilla makes way for busy mysotis.
Allium fireworks explode against the fence
while harebells and hydrangeas lay their cool wrists
on a fever of roses
and brilliant delphiniums coach lilies
to aim ever higher. I love
this river of blue
                    bluer
                          bluest bloom
flowing through the hay-coloured heat-scorched grass
soothing it, and me,
and the browsing, buzzing,
fat-happy
bees!

Aconitum in October, extravagant purple,
a wizard's hat floating among the yellow leaves.
"Monkshood" they call it,
though it's nothing so ascetic or forlorn.
In the beaten-down garden
only the rose-hips' hard brightness
challenge its devil-may-care
its too-late-for-regrets
defiance.

Those rose-hips which,
in their tough little hearts
hold more compacted brilliance
than the easy blossoms
they follow. Late bloomers: late
as in late Brahms. Not tardy
but ripe.

~

Their expiration is callously drawn out—a cascade of loss,
the body shrinking, wrinkling, yellowing,
a leaf-by-leaf amputation until the blackened head
stares blindly at that sun it can no longer follow.

Meanwhile new blooms spring up around the fading ancients,
shouldering them aside: oblivious, heartless, but so beautiful
we instantly forgive them. Life flits from blossom to blossom;
its tongue probes the honey of summer;
it is insatiable.

Those we love we try to coax into staying
but it is not their way, though they swear
never to forget us, and to return bearing new gifts.
We clutch this promise to us through the chill that follows
squinting at the snow, imagining instead
a blizzard of white blossom.

CREDITS

The "Aconitum" section in "In the Garden" and "The Dog at the End of the Bed," *Prairie Fire*

The last section of "Breath" and "Jam," *The New Quarterly*

An earlier version of "Average Life" appeared in *The Antigonish Review* under the title "Corazon"

"Hats," *The Saranac Review* (U.S.)

"Homeopathic Remedies for Scar Tissue," *La Traductière* 29 (France), with a translation by Jacques Rancourt

"Island," *The Fiddlehead*

"Jacob's Ladder," *Rhubarb* and *Shirim*

"Kiss," *Arc*; and also in *La Traductière* 28 (France), with a translation by Marilyn Bertoncini

"Snow," *The Malahat Review*

"Yarrow" was first published in *Common Magic: The Book of the New* (Kingston, Ontario, 2008) and also appeared in the special 35th anniversary issue of *CVII*.

An earlier version of "Breath" was short-listed for the 2009 CBC Radio/ Air Canada Literary Award under the title "Comings and Goings."

"On Finding a Copy of *Pigeon* in the Hospital Bookstore" was shortlisted for the 2011 Montreal Poetry Prize, and appears in *The Global Poetry Anthology* (Signal Editions/Véhicule Press, 2012).

"Things From Which One Never Recovers" was shortlisted for the 2011 Winston Collins/ Descant Prize.

"Yarrow" won an honourable mention in the 2007 Surrey International Writing Competition and was published in their anthology.

ACKNOWLEDGEMENTS

The found poem about poisonous plants in "In the Garden" comes from the Canadian Poisonous Plants Information System, http://www.cbif.gc.ca/pls/pp/poison?p_x=px. "Homeopathic Remedies for Scar Tissue" drew on several different now-forgotten Internet sites, and may well plagiarize other people's formulations, for which both thanks and apologies are due. "Yarrow" inadvertently stole a line from Carolyn Smart.

Thanks to Roo Borson, Helen Dunmore, Jacques Rancourt, and Carolyn Smart for their encouragement of, and response to, earlier versions of some of these poems, and especially to my editor, Carmine Starnino, for his fearless acuity.

Signal
EDITIONS

Carmine Starnino, Editor
Michael Harris, Founding Editor

THE NEW WORLD Carmine Starnino
THE LONG COLD GREEN EVENINGS OF SPRING Elisabeth Harvor
FAULT LINE Laura Lush
WHITE STONE: THE ALICE POEMS Stephanie Bolster
KEEP IT ALL Yves Boisvert (Translated by Judith Cowan)
THE GREEN ALEMBIC Louise Fabiani
THE ISLAND IN WINTER Terence Young
A TINKERS' PICNIC Peter Richardson
SARACEN ISLAND: THE POEMS OF ANDREAS KARAVIS David Solway
BEAUTIES ON MAD RIVER: SELECTED AND NEW POEMS Jan Conn
WIND AND ROOT Brent MacLaine
HISTORIES Andrew Steinmetz
ARABY Eric Ormsby
WORDS THAT WALK IN THE NIGHT Pierre Morency
   (Translated by Lissa Cowan and René Brisebois)
A PICNIC ON ICE: SELECTED POEMS Matthew Sweeney
HELIX: NEW AND SELECTED POEMS John Steffler
HERESIES: THE COMPLETE POEMS OF ANNE WILKINSON, 1924-1961
   Edited by Dean Irvine
CALLING HOME Richard Sanger
FIELDER'S CHOICE Elise Partridge
MERRYBEGOT Mary Dalton
MOUNTAIN TEA Peter Van Toorn
AN ABC OF BELLY WORK Peter Richardson
RUNNING IN PROSPECT CEMETERY Susan Glickman
MIRABEL Pierre Nepveu (Translated by Judith Cowan)
POSTSCRIPT Geoffrey Cook
STANDING WAVE Robert Allen
THERE, THERE Patrick Warner
HOW WE ALL SWIFTLY: THE FIRST SIX BOOKS Don Coles
THE NEW CANON: AN ANTHOLOGY OF CANADIAN POETRY
   Edited by Carmine Starnino
OUT TO DRY IN CAPE BRETON Anita Lahey
RED LEDGER Mary Dalton
REACHING FOR CLEAR David Solway
OX Christopher Patton
THE MECHANICAL BIRD Asa Boxer
SYMPATHY FOR THE COURIERS Peter Richardson
MORNING GOTHIC: NEW AND SELECTED POEMS George Ellenbogen
36 CORNELIAN AVENUE Christopher Wiseman
THE EMPIRE'S MISSING LINKS Walid Bitar
PENNY DREADFUL Shannon Stewart
THE STREAM EXPOSED WITH ALL ITS STONES D.G. Jones
PURE PRODUCT Jason Guriel
ANIMALS OF MY OWN KIND Harry Thurston
BOXING THE COMPASS Richard Greene
CIRCUS Michael Harris
THE CROW'S VOW Susan Briscoe
WHERE WE MIGHT HAVE BEEN Don Coles
MERIDIAN LINE Paul Bélanger (Translated by Judith Cowan)
SPINNING SIDE KICK Anita Lahey
GIFT HORSE Mark Callanan
SUMPTUARY LAWS Nyla Matuk
THE SMOOTH YARROW Susan Glickman